The Quack Quack Song

The Quack Quack Song

SHARON A GREENWAY

Illustrated by Kaylee Chapin

XULON PRESS

Xulon Press
2301 Lucien Way #415
Maitland, FL 32751
407.339.4217
www.xulonpress.com

ISBN-13: 978-1-54565-925-0

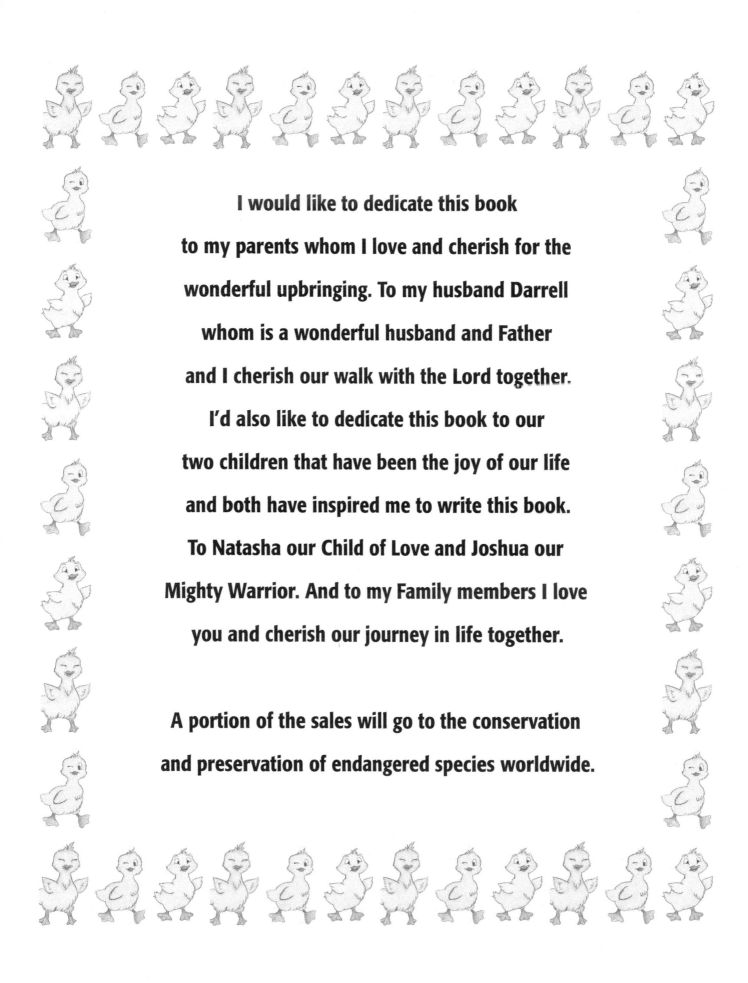

I would like to dedicate this book

to my parents whom I love and cherish for the

wonderful upbringing. To my husband Darrell

whom is a wonderful husband and Father

and I cherish our walk with the Lord together.

I'd also like to dedicate this book to our

two children that have been the joy of our life

and both have inspired me to write this book.

To Natasha our Child of Love and Joshua our

Mighty Warrior. And to my Family members I love

you and cherish our journey in life together.

A portion of the sales will go to the conservation

and preservation of endangered species worldwide.

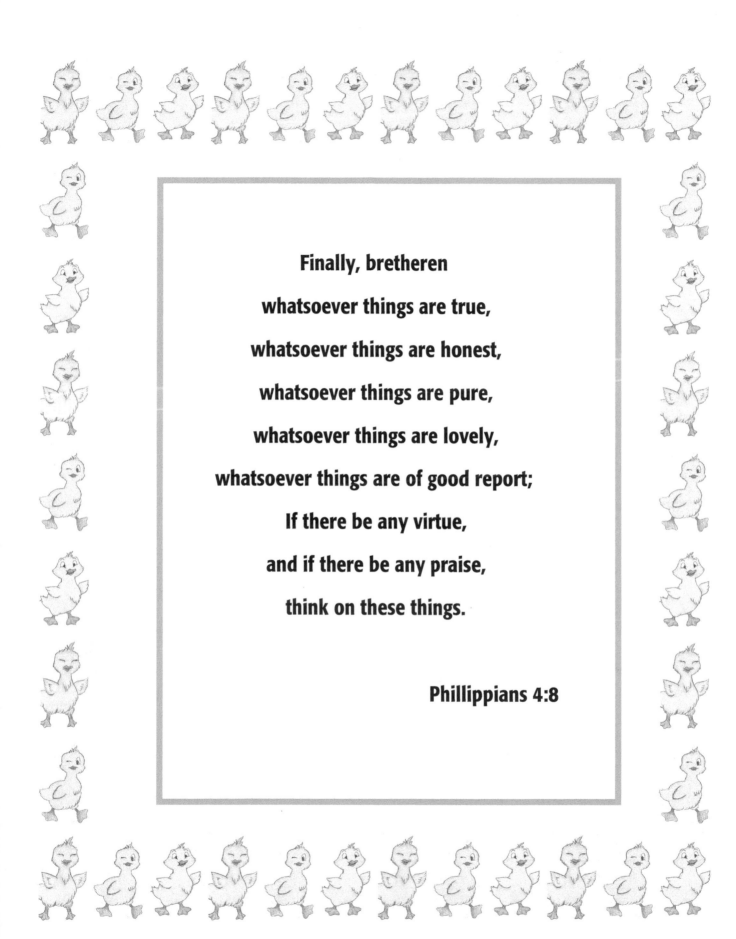

Finally, bretheren

whatsoever things are true,

whatsoever things are honest,

whatsoever things are pure,

whatsoever things are lovely,

whatsoever things are of good report;

If there be any virtue,

and if there be any praise,

think on these things.

Phillippians 4:8

My name is Burt and I'm a silly little Duck,
And I think I have all the bad luck.

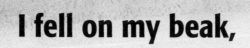

I fell on my beak,

And Oh, it hurts.

But I will not think of that

I'll think about the good things
Quack Quack

(Kids say Quack Quack)

No, I will not think of the bad.
Quack Quack

(Kids say Quack Quack)

It say's in God's word that it rains on the just,

And the unjust that means us all.

So instead of sitting down,
And soaking in my troubles,
I'll just get up and have a ball

And I'll Think about the good things
Quack Quack
(Kids say Quack Quack)

I'll Think about the good things
Quack Quack

(Kids say Quack Quack)

I'll Think about the good things
Quack Quack

(Kids say Quack Quack)

No, I will not think of the bad Quack Quack

(Kids say Quack Quack)

Invitation to The Prayer of Salvation

Here are a few scriptures on Salvation.

In John 3:16, Romans 10:13, Romans 10:9-10, Acts 16:31, Acts 2:21 and Revelations 3:20 The Bible says if we believe in our hearts and confess with our mouth we shall be saved. We would like to invite you to say this simple prayer of Salvation. If you would like to be saved and you will go to Heaven for ever.

Dear God,

Thank you for loving me and for sending your Son to die for my sins. I'm sorry for my sins and I receive Jesus Christ as my savior. Now as your child I turn my entire life over to you.

Amen

Reference to scripture with additional verses for you to Think About the Good Things .

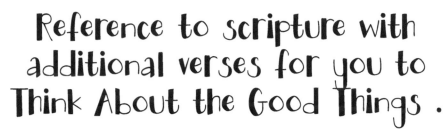

1. **Matthew 5:45**

That you may be the children of your Father which is in heaven: for he maketh his sun to rise on the evil and on the good and sendeth rain on the just and the unjust

2. **Romans 8:28**

And we know that all things work together for good to them that love God, to them who are the called according to his purpose.

3. **Jeremiah 29:11**

For I know the plans I have for you," declares the Lord "plans to prosper you and not to harm you, plans to give you hope and a future.

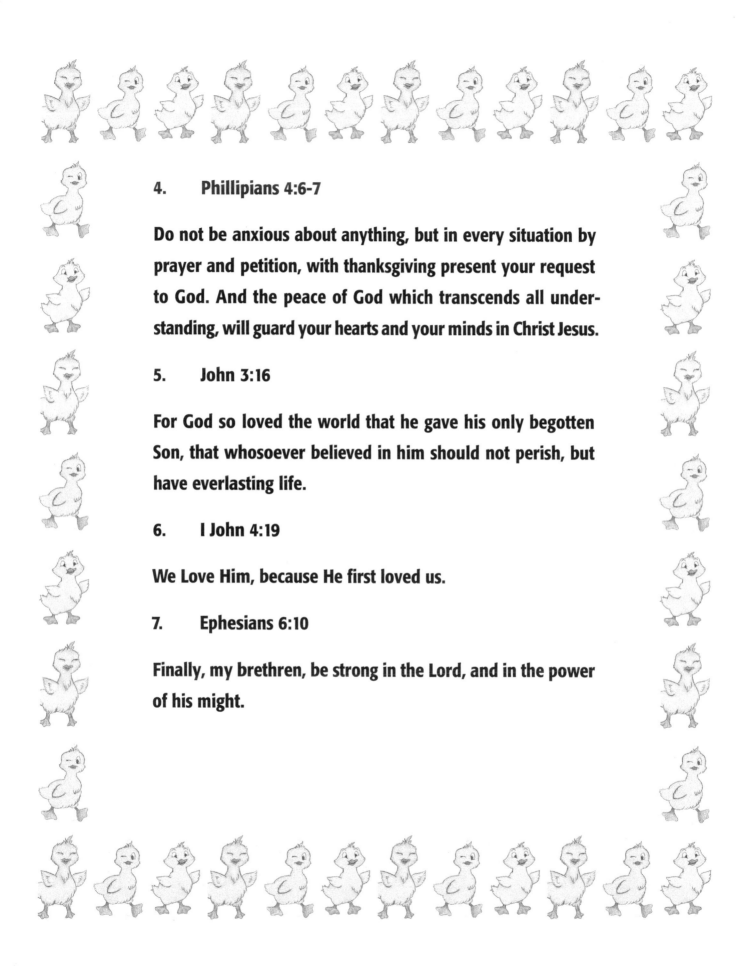

4.   **Phillipians 4:6-7**

Do not be anxious about anything, but in every situation by prayer and petition, with thanksgiving present your request to God. And the peace of God which transcends all understanding, will guard your hearts and your minds in Christ Jesus.

5.   **John 3:16**

For God so loved the world that he gave his only begotten Son, that whosoever believed in him should not perish, but have everlasting life.

6.   **I John 4:19**

We Love Him, because He first loved us.

7.   **Ephesians 6:10**

Finally, my brethren, be strong in the Lord, and in the power of his might.

CPSIA information can be obtained
at www.ICGtesting.com
Printed in the USA
BVHW022005090419
545085BV00008B/22/P

9 781545 659250